points of balance
pablo medina
puntos de apoyo

Also by PABLO MEDINA

Poetry

Puntos de apoyo

The Floating Island

Arching into the Afterlife

Pork Rind and Cuban Songs

Fiction

The Cigar Roller

The Return of Félix Nogara

The Marks of Birth

Memoir

Exiled Memories: A Cuban Childhood

Translation

Everyone Will Have to Listen:
The Poetry of Tania Díaz Castro
(editor and translator, with C. Hospital)

points of balance
pablo medina
puntos de apoyo

Four Way Books
New York City

Distributed by
University Press of New England
Hanover and London

Editorial Office
Four Way Books
POB 535, Village Station
New York, NY 10014
www.fourwaybooks.com

Library of Congress Catalogue Card Number: 2004101058

ISBN 1-884800-64-5

Cover Art: Pablo A. Medina (Jr.)

Book Design: Pablo A. Medina (Jr.) and Margarita Mayoral-Medina

Typefaces: Farnham Text and Farnham Italic designed by Christian Schwartz

This book is manufactured in the United States of America and printed on
acid-free paper.

**NATIONAL
ENDOWMENT
FOR THE ARTS**
Publication of this book is made possible in part by an award
from the National Endowment for the Arts, which believes that
a great nation deserves great art, and by a generous grant from a
private foundation.

This publication is also made possible with a regrant from the Council of
Literary Magazines and Presses, supported by public funds from the New
York State Council of the Arts, a state agency.

Four Way Books is a not-for-profit organization. We are grateful for the
assistance we receive from individual donors, foundations, and government
arts agencies.

Distributed by University Press of New England
One Court Street, Lebanon, NH 03766

ACKNOWLEDGMENTS

Some of the poems in the collection have appeared or are about to appear in the following magazines: *Artful Dodge, Barrow Street, A Gathering of the Tribes, Global City Review, Linden Lane Magazine, Marlboro Review, Minimus, New York Quarterly, Plum Review, and Rattapallax.*

Poems published in anthologies:

"Intertext," "The Pillars of Community," "Tectonics of the Imperceptible," "Purpose and Extravagance," "Rearview," and "Vegetable Tantra" were first published in *Shade 2004,* (Four Way Books, New York: 2003).

"Havana Dream," "Amor Vincit Omnia," "Venus in Varadero," "The Peasant Heart," "Before the Solutions," and "End of the Affair" were first published in *Hammer and Blaze: A Gathering of American Poets,* (University of Georgia Press, Athens, GA: 2002).

The Spanish *fulcros* were originally collected in *Puntos de apoyo,* Editorial Betania, Madrid: 2002.

for Beth

THE FULCRUM

One day after I had been writing prose for months, the thought occurred to me that my poet-self would die if I did not write a poem. I moved away from the computer and sat with notebook and pen. What came was a six-line piece in Spanish. I tried again a few hours later and came up with another six-line poem, this time in English. Over the next few days, I forgot all about prose and wrote what I eventually called fulcrums at a furious pace, in both languages. At times I was totally unaware of what tongue I was using, so effective was the form, so unencumbered by the preconceptions that we bring to the writing of poems. The fulcrum was not only keeping my poet-self alive in both languages, but making it leap with excitement out of the water of its lethargy.

The fulcrum—or fulcro in Spanish—is a six-line poem divided into unrhymed couplets with a syntactic/semantic shift in the middle stanza. The structure is reminiscent of the Taoist hexagram. It is a meeting of chance and form, spontaneity and shape, movement and stasis. It combines the dialectic of the sonnet with the imagistic power of the haiku but is free of either tradition, its primary intent being the shaping of language and silence into a point of balance floating in the ocean of time.

TABLE OF CONTENTS

PUNTOS DE APOYO

PUNTOS DE APOYO

Note: The poems in this book are not translations but, rather, reflections of each other. The book can be read in English, in Spanish, or, ideally, as it was written, concurrently in both languages.

Where will I find a bell that sounds inside your dreams?
—Pablo Neruda

Swimming light, will you come now?
—Paul Celan

MIRAGE

I move from one language
to another, I dive

from a pool of water
to a pool of dreams,

from the fire of words
to the shadow beyond them.

5

REPRODUCCIÓN

Un solo pájaro vuela
al noroeste.

El sol se pone
como se pone un huevo,

con gran pujanza
y mayor desaliento.

6

THE COMPLICITY OF THE FAMILIAR

Love is
the grammar of solitude.

I turn on the radio,
a neighbor knocks at the door,

I multiply the distance
between me and desire.

7

PERRO EN TRES PARTES

Primero, la cola metrónoma,
andante con brío.

Segundo, el torso nervioso,
color de miel con pulgas.

Tercero, la cara triste,
desierta de ironía.

8

LADY WITH A DOG

When the strange dog came
to her I knew I

wanted her as much—
red sun, red moon,

skin like a snow field
on fire.

9

PASACALLE

Castañuelas, relicarios,
todo eso se aguarda.

Ahinco a la musa,
torrencial de cariño,

con sus pestañas
de aliento y agua fuerte.

THE TRANSMUTATION OF SUBSTANCES

Two ducks are copulating
on the snow.

I slide downhill on a steam iron.
There are no hills,

there is no snow. The streetlight
makes everything dark.

EL SÍ DE LAS NIÑAS

Andan de un lado a otro
mascando chicle, soltando risas.

Sus caderas suenan como campanas,
sus olores son veinte mares,

en sus miradas mueren los años
y saltan los derviches

CITYSCAPE 1

Let the aroma of need
waft across the river to New Jersey:

all the snow and hills,
a sky that moves and moves.

I saw a rose in the clouds,
I saw happiness on fire.

SISTEMA CERRADO

Al romperse la botella
brotó la nostalgia del eterno retorno,

largas playas,
cangrejos complacientes,

marinero de los calcios
enyugado a la noria del mar.

14

FACT AND FAMINE

The streets are filled with non-cars,
non-buildings, non-people.

I think of your face
through the waste and the crowds

(hungry, impeded), the thousand
shards of sleep between us.

EL MARTIRIO DE EMPÉDOCLES

Ese animal de huesos
grises y lengua áspera,

ese desperdicio de las sandalias,
saltó a la caldera de la historia,

pero sin estrépito y con las grandes
aspiraciones de la manteca.

TOURNIQUETS AND ALL

The little self grew big,
the narrow curve relented.

You sliced into the butter of my longing.
Then. Now? The island

flashes like a knife, the dead
are swimming in my shadow.

CIUDADELA

Caja caudal de números
impares. La cábala interfiere.

En el mar los peces duermen.
Ofuscan las intemperies.

Cópulo airoso (el imperio),
puerta abierta (maleza).

INTERREGNUM

My rivering brown,
my sweet stand against the city,

like this love between us:
the fracture and fall,

the smoke rising,
the beginning of ruin.

LA ZOZOBRA EN NUEVA YORK

Me han quitado los espejos,
esa manera de vivir con lo posible,

de imaginarme un adefesio
(suspiro submarino,

sofoco oxigenado), esa manera
de aullar desde la luna.

20

CITYSCAPE 2

The glandular air
of November sweeps through

with little to offer
except the Hudson at five o'clock,

the black ships passing,
the lights of Verrazano on the map.

LA SOMBRA DE BÍPEDO QUE ME PERSIGUE

De día y de noche (una luz)
tras los pasos negros

de un atónito (respiraciones),
juego de naipes,

rey de oro, as de espada,
el derrumbe de la madrugada.

THE PILLARS OF COMMUNITY

Two leather money belts
hung around the bony hips.

They are like illness and joy
(how fat, how frantic),

dirty blond who smells armpits,
metal mouth that eats ham bones.

TRAVESÍA

Fíjense como suenan
los camiones

con esas ansias
de yo-no-fui.

¡Cuántos niños devorados!
¡Y los gemidos de padre!

PURPOSE AND EXTRAVAGANCE

Wounded cross
and the statuary of broken angels,

I am open hearted.
Into me swing your wrecking

ball, your arraignments. I am yours
forever, plane-encrusted.

EL SITIO DE LAS RUINAS

Empecemos con la sangre
que nos asfixia.

Llega una voz de madre (muda).
Se espanta.

Al fin cae la tarde. Se reúnen
los huecos a cacarear.

CITYSCAPE 3

A red light over the city,
our solitudes ringing.

Here I am (an interval),
there you are (an equinox).

We go where the wind grows.
We enter the hollows of autumn.

ISLA PORTENTOSA

Camarada de los tuertos,
despiértame (anúnciame)

el anhelo de la tumba,
la floresta de intuiciones.

Un yo parlante camina
hacia la llama.

DRESS REHEARSAL

This city is a French
horn in distress.

Calvin chasing hens
and the pages of the hymnal blank

like a furious whoosh,
a stomach pain, the pitch of sin.

LA LLANURA DEL TIEMPO

Érase una niña
con mirada de pato.

Se cerró el año
con cifras y cuernos.

Y nos llegó el futuro,
un cuacuá, una sonrisa entumecida.

THE GEOMETRIES OF SUMMER

The insinuation of flesh and leg—
I say no more,

who wants silence.
A woman bends to pick up the wind,

fends off the broken circuits:
desire (spin, grow).

31

PROYECTO DE LUYANÓ

Gallinero operático
con música de alto solar.

Por la acera se pasean
dos mulatas irónicas, babilónicas.

Alegoría y sopor, perlas (leche y cal)
deseo de echarse al mar.

32

HAD WE MORE PARADISE

Had we more paradise
it would be reachable in the imagining.

Behold a still-life permanence:
a saw cutting wood, a woodthrush

calling, a quietude that grieves even
as it teaches us longing, return.

33

EL ABISMO DE LAS AVES

Ahí caemos todos,
en esa gran oscuridad

(canturreo de las aves,
revoloteo en un fondo gris)—

chirrí, chirrí sin salida, sin saber
si es eterna la alegría o el horror.

34

CITYSCAPE 4

The heart fast beating,
tenure of grief, of unknowing.

Bird swoops out of the cliffs
to the old factory.

Stranded on the next page
the arthropod sun is rising.

ANIMULA BLANDULA VAGULA

Brújula esdrújula (súbita),
cantera de sienes y cementerios.

Mandrágora tántrica encárnase,
(viuda loca) huele a pierna

con tiñosa,
salado imperio, indagado sol.

THE RIVER

Laughter is a found song,
a pine tree after winter,

figures in the shallows with poles,
Camden, Philadelphia,

then a brown death opening
which is the sea.

LLOVIZNA

La luz es clara pero gris.
Londrecita, terca, ensimismada.

En el parque
hay un silencio de calcetín.

En la cama hay
olor a inglés, búho alazán.

38

SAMADHI

The blessing time
and the damning time

dancing all around,
palm trees in the garden,

lemons for lemonade,
three moons asleep on the snow.

LUEGO SOY

Laberinto Dios,
pez antropófago.

Tal vez me llama la ausencia,
yegua relinchona.

Se destiñe el espejo:
desaparezco yo.

40

WAKING SLOW

To a moth-replacement
for the gauze of flesh,

dangerous to the degree of object
without dreaming, odors without closure.

I give a present to myself:
smeared language.

ALEVOSÍA Y PASIÓN

Antes que la luna brincara
había un estrépito constante

(fanfarrón de sapo). Fría allí
la lengua de los santos

que lo añoraban todo:
mesura, placer, desilusión.

42

PASTORAL

The rain has rhythm
and dusk comes slithering

like smoke, like snake,
a climbing vine. Shepherd?

Shepherd asks for love.
The answer is the sea.

MANUAL DE INSTRUCCIONES

Mírate en el paisaje
de diez melancolías.

Encala tu cuerpo de extranjero
a cuatro alas

y que la isla que llevas a los hombros
se convierta en mediodía.

44

EX LIBRIS

Childhood was Cervantes,
adulthood flared with Hemingway.

I look for death in every book,
intertextual, salivary:

what the ocean says
and says again and then forgets.

ASTOR PIAZZOLLA

Ese hombre oblicuo
tiene manos de oprobio.

Buenos Aires arde,
súbita, sexual.

Los bandoneones
apestan a Dios.

VERSE LIBRE

Watching blue sky,
red leaves, he

finds an aesthetic:
how little he loves

the world, not the thing
but the idea.

COMPOSICIÓN EN ALTA MAR

Nefasto, incierto te lo digo:
los tres lobos marinos

que nos persiguen
no son más

que un mal entendimiento
entre el amor y la muerte.

JARCHA: EL AMOR PASA

Love happens like a shadow
over a sleeping town.

I have a slit on my belly
through which a child could pass.

A bird drops three tiny seeds.
A plane purrs overhead.

49

SALÓN LEZAMIANO

Leves alegorías de retóricas flores
perturban la paz de los alfileres.

Un sátrapa (hediondo, cosquillón)
pregona el amor. Su mujer

(costurera que mucho sabe)
contesta: ¡Destripador!

50

ARS POETICA

What do you know
about poetry?

What do you know
about the last grain

of the last meal of rice
on the universe of your plate?

51

LA PALABRITA

Así va, poquito a poco,
de una encía a la otra.

Por aquí se entra al mar,
eso dijo la corneta.

Por aquí se llega a la vejiga,
aclaró el amanecer.

DEBUSSY

Watch it, let it go, then piano
broken burst a fly and water

fell through flax. No,
but it was soft and it was loud

and it roamed into a place
that moans in musk.

EL GALÁN DE LOS TABURETES

Tornose avestruz (patiflojo),
danzonete interpretado entre las nieves.

Así es la nostalgia,
igual que la isla en su candor:

confusión de formas,
ola rota en el umbral.

RUSSIAN DOLL

Every wall is an eye,
every eye is a wall.

I have only myself tonight
in a language inside a language

about the white sky falling
and the black earth.

NOSTALGIA DE LA AUSENCIA

La laguna en la mañana
cruje con su afán de mar.

María, ten piedad
(¡cómo insisten los cristianos!).

Yo no digo nada.
La playa más amplia es el silencio.

SHIBBOLETH OF CENTRAL PARK

In my throat is a word
(unsaid) like the wind

sanctioning a memory:
a woman gnawing bones,

her green eyes
my mind's astonishment.

EROS Y TANATOS

Esta mañana desperté
con fango en las venas.

El reloj decía las seis.
El sexo pululaba.

La muerte me lamía el vientre
y el amor a mil leguas.

TEMPERANCE

Red in the park,
vulvas and delineations.

I remember the sunrise
opening

and a redolent coin
and a sublime insertion.

PRIAPO

Hombrecito cabezón
empinado hacia el noroeste.

Nunca gimió la madre
su transfiguración inerte,

nunca escucharon los talmúdicos
su voz de niña sin dientes.

BREVIARY

And when I run out of things
to say, what do I say?

And when the thrush sings
in the know-it-all woods,

isn't there a slippage
from language to departure?

61

A PRUEBA DE BALAS

Petronio blindado
con su sexo a cuestas.

Tenemos que llenar las tinas,
asistir a los suicidios.

Poco a poco se nos va la sangre,
se hace tumba, son, tentáculo.

INTERTEXT

I throw a rose on the street
and wait for the car (with you in it).

My rose (bruised)
prettifying the oil slicks

and you in the car, blond, fast
like solar wind (chasing dawn).

63

CAPRICHO

Suerte de estar perdido
en los suburbios.

Los autos arden
como en el cine.

Aparece la carroza blanca.
Trae a la doncella que sabe a sal(v)ación.

64

NOSTALGIA

Distance is (of mirrors)
the most derisive mother,

there on the shorn horizon,
green island, shore-brow.

The sun sets over the humming sea
into a sieve called other.

65

PARÁFRASIS

Ropa al viento, tarde lenta, el perro
ladra en casa del vecino.

¿Cómo es que entramos
a esta confección?

Somos viejos.
Un nido de caderas nos espera.

LAST RITE

At eighty-one and smiling
my uncle told everyone

he was going
to die. I can still

get it up, he said,
but it bends.

TIEMPO FRÍO

Al fondo del lago
dos gorriones entran y salen

de la ortiga. Un niño los persigue.
Tiempo frío, fría tierra.

Me arde la cara. Una memoria:
el viento es una llama.

ONE SIZE FITS ALL

So far the breeze is steady,
languor and twirl from the south,

then the day turns sodden, holds
its breath. The branches

of the willow stir:
a woman coughs in her soup.

VENCIDO DE LA EDAD

Todo me envuelve en el silencio
de las aguas de la desdicha:

ocho pezones de perra,
las tres rabias de un valiente,

un tomeguín cantando
un aire frío, mal interpretado.

PLUTONIC TONIC

Oh death, the beeper says
and cautionary ashes falling.

Deodorant (cloud passing)
between me and memory:

slowly the faucet drips,
(slowly) the shadow waxes.

ELEGÍA CORTA

Belarmina calcinada,
madre de las cenizas,

anda por los cielos
oliendo a tumba atolondrada,

de manos con el viento
sobre almejas y desventajas.

APOTHEGM TO TACITUS

All the wars of the world
are in my veins. Stand fast,

a woman is weeping,
(stand fast) desolation comes

disguised as darkness
and they call it peace.

EL PAN DE CADA DÍA

Ruido de esparto,
figura de gato.

Así entra el viento,
escapa la soledad,

ámbito, estrépito,
ayer renuente, corva realidad.

74

THE GLOBAL ECONOMY: LESSON ONE

Pomegranates for the hogs
feeding where the night

gives birth to fear
and fear to blindness:

an eye in an empty bucket
looking to find the moon.

TRISTE TRÓPICO

Lo que vemos
son los escombros del mar,

la ideología, esa niña
perdida en una gran mentira,

y un patriarca alardoso
disputando con el sol.

PORK BARREL

The libertarian economists
and the moralist right

are banding together.
Bring out the grape juice!

Practice your golf swing!
The earth movers are eating the fields.

MAL TIEMPO

Agravio, amigo,
¡cuánta falta me has hecho!

Ayer fue un día glacial.
Anduve descalzo,

se me empaparon las cejas,
el mundo se hizo almidón.

RITES OF SPRING

Rain, cold morning,
a mother dead, a father aging:

numbers like steps,
numbers like wakings,

a slight green tint to the trees,
the growing tenderness of branches.

79

LA TERNURA DE LA PIEDRA

Es cuarzo maternal, suspiro
de la luna internada

en sal. Glóbulo,
llama de dos vientres,

sueño de lagartos tenues
a la entrada del mar.

80

AMOR VINCIT OMNIA

So this is where the cunning
coney lives.

Look at it come close, go far,
cross highways, reach the sea,

its ambidextrous eyes
leaping (perpendicular) like fish.

SUBTERFUGIO ENTRE TÚ Y YO

Cuando nació la luna
le dio albergue el río.

Catafalco de los suspiros (yo),
tú (eremita) devolviéndome

la noche. Tú (interpretada)
saltimbanque de las nieves.

MATINAL

This morning I sense solution,
I sense inference.

All sounds conspire to euphony.
The clock moves

as the heart moves
in one direction: silence.

NOCHE DE RONDAS

Esta noche se caducan
los trastos, la luna cae

(adivina) pendiente de tus ojos.
Esta noche acosa el bien:

palabreo, viento, deslumbre,
el vello de tu vientre en soledad.

TECTONICS OF THE IMPERCEPTIBLE

I sit at my desk
waiting for you.

My heart (quick hound)
jumps to a memory:

blue land (your face),
around it the ocean of sleep.

PAISAJE CON PAPALOTE

Cuando te quise te quise
de mar abierto

con la esperanza del solitario,
en mi desnudez (diastólica),

en mi pensamiento de papalote:
pecho al viento (arcilla, luz).

LEAKY FAUCET

Drip by drip by drain by drown,
this is the torrent felicity.

Look at the fish low
(wangled, sententious).

Look at the cows float (tensile,
pursuant). They water.

EL GRAN COMER

Mi sueño fue arduo, pentecostal.
Y cuando se abrieron las grietas

de la hambruna, me acordé
de los toldos del mercado,

todo aquel sol (como un banquete)
y el olor a cachimba natal.

VEGETABLE TANTRA

You are okra to me,
you are vegetable stew,

seed pod, tomato
in a clandestine pot.

Remember how you nourished me
and I whirled like a dervishe.

89

INVENCIÓN EN TRES PARTES

Presiento bajo el mar
una esplanada de sueño (blanco, carnal).

Atiendo entre las cabrillas
el suspiro antifonal

de una malquerida
(¿y por qué no?) atisbada.

REARVIEW

I am alone (weep for me)
inside a car in Iowa.

My lover (hills on her mind)
has left me for an alpinist

with money and muscles.
The mirror trembles (illusion).

CARTOGRAFÍA

¿Cómo hilvanar el deseo
con la distancia, la distancia

con su plumaje de rara ave?
¿Cómo trazar esos muslos

de luna llena, ese monte de labios
sabios, ese sueño de isla almagre?

HAVANA DREAM

The red eye blinks and it is you
(in between the rain)

out of the crumbling rooms,
a note played on the piano,

a salt wind off the ocean,
lonely, refracted (you).

93

LOS PAÍSES BAJOS

Tanto pasa entre un vaso roto
y un garrafón de estruendo,

un mameluco, un escarabajo.
Sobre la tumba de los ciegos

hay un aire de pechos grises,
una caquita de centauro.

94

NEW TANGO

Not those old places
(not the strain of abandon).

You want to rob the present
for childhood, the streets

for the crust of a dream
where your voice comes back in a bell.

95

LA HABANA A LA DERIVA

Los muslos brotan del deseo
como las flores del anochecer.

Atenuación de los lunares
(el no pertenecer): sale ella al balcón

descalza, chupándose los dedos.
Poco a poco nos hacemos mar.

CAPRICE

Happiness is a sheet
in the wind (the flap of it).

What you did,
what you did not do,

a sip of beer, our lips
barely brushing.

97

PERISCOPIO SENTIMENTAL #3

Así como la lluvia
es mar y el mar anillo,

así como la luna es aullido
(mal de amor), así

eres tú, tal como los ecos tendidos,
mordidos (en flor).

EMBLEM AND ENCOMIUM

Listen to the cousin's voice
inside the frog. Find yourself

where the light has a green reach,
intrigue of in-between

the notes (there, aptly)
the pumice of dreams.

BOCANADA DE ASTUCIAS

Sombras elefantes
en la utopía de la ambigüedad.

Y por todo y ante todo
resuena la clave (muda maravillosa),

hojas cojas, cielo tañido,
cascabel de cal.

TECHNIQUE OF WHAT

What is the snow
and flotsam on the bed?

What is the flatness of waking?
What are the dry throats of starlings

(quick, cowardly)
calling for, greenery or death?

PECERA DE LOS ÁNIMOS

Decir pez es como decir
señor en su dominio,

como decir buzo (corazón)
en su actitud de Nemo,

caracol (vientre)
pastando entre las algas.

106

THE PLASMA EFFECT

Cross from moment to cloud
the landscape of trifles,

the stare of cows (languid)
in an afternoon of sustenance,

the dull linkages
of mastic and violence.

LA VERDAD EN SI BEMOL

Al despertar no había inteligencia
sino la caja de kleenex

en la mesa de noche (casi vacía),
y el sueño de un hijo

mordiendo una manzana
(casi entera).

ALL HALLOWS

Jackhammers, backhoes,
smell of men digging

the lake of relentlessness.
My fear stands at the shore

of your leaving. A fish
jumps out of your eyes.

PUNTILLISMO FAROLERO

Garza flaca la del boticario
que se toma la cerveza por tonel.

Desea a la vecina,
se rompe el taburete,

nalgas vagas, cascabel
(amor) domado, olor a pie.

FIRST FROST

How will it seem now,
the arrival of majestic December?

Dribble of rain,
the cold clapping in,

you miles away
in your casements.

SÚCUBO

Perra ampulosa,
lengua afuera

y mancha negra en el hocico.
Yo dormido

pero con entusiasmo
y con la inocencia a medias.

THE PEASANT HEART

At dusk the snow turns blue,
the moon yawns to frigid black.

And you? Bone long
and deep to the south.

I wanted song (return).
I had the knowledge of never.

ÍNCUBO

¿Quién es quién?
Chancho a la hembra,

siempre con música, buen vino,
ella bella durmiente,

él con ese olor a manteca,
tocino indolente.

114

THE FIXED MARK

I was not restrainful.
I was not indoctrinated.

Love is love that alters
and bends and ends and grows

(again) the bridge from my lips
to the flagon of desire.

ABEJÓN SINFÓNICO

Alvéolo tangente
(lavándome las manos)

(remendando tumbas),
perspícate o seré yo

quien te adumbre,
so mefítico, so contumaz.

BEFORE THE SOLUTIONS

In the boxes a year's supply
of moods (bovine, sublunary).

I hear them out,
I hear them in.

New tone on the street,
new tone, same boxes.

VENUS EN VARADERO

El mar es de muchas mentes.
Una es música, otra

se adhiere al silencio.
La última es rubia, delgada,

el pelo hecho labios con el viento
(tilde al revés).

AFFLICTION

Sometimes knowledge will
warm you like a glove,

sometimes you want to storm
the gates of forgetting.

Oh lizard eyes! Oh my containment,
swallow the ashes!

CARIBEOSIDAD

Un archipiélago fosforecente
me constata.

El niño busca en la isla
un manojo de alas.

No ve los sueños,
 no se aferra de los montes.

120

VENUS IN VARADERO

The sea is chaste with many minds.
One is naked (she walks

out of the waves). Another
invented silence (her hair becomes

the wind). The third remembers
the music (before it was a song).

EL CUBANO Y SUS INDICIOS

Dentro de la soledad
se abrazan cuatro exilios:

el viento en la negrura,
un radio que ha perdido el círculo,

el sur aplanado en nieve,
el poeta en busca del lenguaje.

SMOKE AND MIRRORS IN HAVANA

The sea in its immensity
is telling a story.

Here is darkness (long,
long train through the night).

There under the carpet, grandmother
dust, grandfather consequence.

LOS APETITOS DEL MAR

Hoy conozco el mal y el bien,
la causa esfinge de los pétalos

del yodo. Hoy me encuentro
incauto, divisorio entre las olas,

confluyendo esquemas,
apaciguando tigres.

A DICTIONARY OF GUATEMALAN BIRD CALLS

In the market a young girl
is selling entrails (boreal,

membranous). The ambiguities
are singing in my ear:

sunset means a crow. City
means Quetzaltenango drowning.

YA SÉ TODAS LAS VERDADES

Cada aliento es metamorfosis,
cada medida es ciclón.

Despertar es estertor.
¿Y si me quedo? ¿Y si me voy?

Corazón (ya sé) tambor famélico
que hace bailar la ilusión.

A TENTACLE APPROACHING THE OBVIOUS

Assail, assail,
there is little time for quizzicals.

Blessed be Ilium.
(You said brilliantine?)

I mean nothing that is,
I mean bob on the sea.

VISTA DE LA HABANA

¡Cómo lo devora todo el sol!
Y se esparce (agua negra) el mal sabor

de un paraíso (a tientas) derrumbado.
En la sombra de un portal

hay un pilar de sal.
En su vientre el mar, el infinito mar.

PABLO MEDINA lived in Havana, Cuba, the first twelve years of his life then moved with his family to New York City, where his culture shock was softened by snow and countless visits to the New York Public Library. He is the author of four previous collections of poetry, three novels, a memoir, and a book of translations, and his work has appeared in periodicals and anthologies in the United States and abroad. Medina has received several awards for his work, among them grants from the Lila Wallace–Reader's Digest Fund, the National Endowment for the Arts, and the Rockefeller Foundation. He lives in New York City with his wife Beth and is on the writing faculties of the New School University and the MFA Program for Writers at Warren Wilson College.